bosses who
KILL

Kimbretta Clay © 2017
Bosses Who Kill: Six Toxic Leadership Behaviors
First Edition, January 2017
KayAvi Press Publishing
Jacksonville, Florida

Author: Kimbretta Clay, Kimbretta.com
Managing Editor: Shayla Eaton, CuriouserEditing.com
Publishing and Design Services: Melinda Martin, MelindaMartin.me

ISBN: 978-0-9989109-0-1 (print), 978-0-9989109-1-8 (epub)

bosses who KILL

SIX TOXIC LEADERSHIP BEHAVIORS

KIMBRETTA CLAY

DEDICATION

To Avion Elisse,
my one true love,
the one who has never left my side,
always believed in me,
encourages me,
loves me unconditionally,
and is my biggest fan.

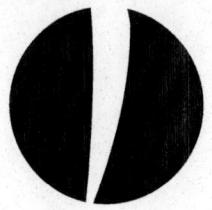

CONTENTS

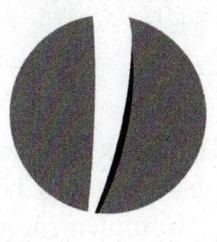

INTRODUCTION

Ignorance is not bliss when it comes to leadership. *Loyalty* and *business* can no longer be used in the same sentence. They do not run parallel to each other anymore, assuming they ever did. There was a time when people would work for the same company over thirty years (my stepdad did); they knew each other's families, prayed for each other during hard times, and felt secure. They had a core belief that if they showed up and did their jobs well, they would have that job for as long as they needed.

A company stood with the people they employed, and the employees could expect to be given raises and advances within the organization.

It is completely opposite today. College students are being taught by mentors and career professionals to leave a company within three to five years after mastering a skill or system, because after all, the only way to advance financially is as a skilled new hire at a new company. People are also being coached to choose a boss and not a job, because a bad boss for someone new to the workforce could alter their entire professional future. I am glad to learn that people are saying out loud, "Hey, choose a good boss." However, they shouldn't have to choose a good boss over a good job, good company, ideal location, or other things one typically looks in to when starting a new career.

In this book, we will explore, analyze, and uncover toxic bad boss personalities and behaviors that are widespread in the professional world. These poisonous behaviors cost money—

that's the bottom line. Hiring executives should spend enough time interviewing and observing new bosses to ensure they fit into their role, even up to implementing at-will probationary hire periods and doing psychological evaluations. In short, hold bad bosses accountable to their bad boss behaviors and give them the tools and resources they need to be good bosses.

I've interviewed over one hundred people, asking them to describe their best and worst boss ever—men, women, and children of various backgrounds, across a multitude of professional fields and sectors, both public and private. As you read this book, you'll see highlights and lowlights of some of those interviews. It came as no surprise to me that everyone has had multiple bad bosses in their professional lifetime and could only recant one or two people they would consider a good boss. I also researched Gallup polls, surveys, blogs, and other written archives describing experiences with bosses at work.

One Gallup poll of over one million people revealed the number-one reason people quit their jobs: because of a bad boss or overall bad leadership. In short, people leave bosses or management, not companies.[1]

Bad bosses bully and abuse their staff because they can, because no one is doing anything about it. Because there has been little to no training on how to motivate, lead, inspire, and develop a group of people. There is rarely any accountability regarding the consistent practice of quality leadership skills; when there is, it is usually regarding quantity of the work being done (output/productivity) and a measurement of gains from said quantity (income) of the individuals doing the work. Mainly because the head of these organizations did not submit to the training themselves, so they cannot hold their staff leaders accountable to training and skills they themselves haven't gained.

I compare bad bosses to serial killers for the basis of this book. So it's only fitting that we research the mindset of a serial killer. I came across a subject matter expert online, Shirley Lynn

Scott, who wrote an informative article about the mindset of a serial killer, called, "What Makes Serial Killers Tick?"[2] Among other research, I found interesting facts and perspectives as well. Shirley and other experts on the subject have stated that the main traits of a psychopath can be defined as follows:

> *"a callous, exploitive individual with blunted emotions, impulsive inclinations, and an inability to feel guilt or remorse."*

I believe we are in the midst of a serial killer epidemic in corporate America, and I would even say this same epidemic has spread throughout our nation across all professional sectors. When it comes to the new-aged serial killers, they come dressed as bosses (i.e., people of authority) and are giving Oscar-winning performances day in and day out as they slaughter people in plain view.

We need to implement hard, consistent, natural consequences—and quickly. If you abuse your authority, it is taken away—period. Either you know how to lead a group of people to individual or group successes, or you don't.

My ultimate goal is to uncover these serial killer bosses, thereby inciting a wake-up call so we can begin the necessary cleanup and transformation of today's leaders, and teach them how to succeed as a good boss in any workplace.

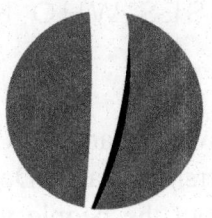

CHAPTER ONE

Thou Shalt Not Kill a Subordinate

"Rank does not confer privilege or give power.
It imposes responsibility."

—*Peter Drucker*

I've always desired to motivate forward movement. I exist to serve. I help others become their best self. These passions within me had consistently been ignored by those who've had the opportunity to lead me in every area of my life, both professionally and personally. Too many people and organizations are in neutral, and they don't even know it.

Training isn't prioritized, and the training that *is* required is centered on processes and procedural updates. Training of management staff on managing people is infrequent, nonexistent, or lacks quality or follow-through. Sure, several businesses have the trainings "available," but I've seen firsthand that very few actually participate in them. Workplace culture says the work *always* comes before the training, so if there's work to do, you can bet no one will be in training.

Businesses can be mechanic: sometimes practicing a use-them-up-and-cut-them-loose method. Employees can be laid off before becoming a tenured financial obligation, given poor severance packages, replaced by someone whose new starting pay is $20,000 less than what they were paying the previous employee.

Businesses are insane, doing the same thing over and over, expecting different results. When does the lightbulb come on for leaders, business owners, and CEOs across our country? Transform your leadership staff! Do something different, like actually caring about the people you employ. Then your business can function and grow, minus the frequent, costly, sometimes life-altering setbacks.

For those who have ever been left behind after a company layoff, you know the amount of work didn't decrease because the staff did. The former employees' work is simply added to the workload of those left behind. While it may appear they save money in salaries, they pay the difference in correcting the errors of those being overworked. Sometimes they pay the difference in the up-training of new hires. While they may have lower salaries than the previous employee, they are still untrained. The setbacks are usually experienced by those who were laid off—even how they respond to those setbacks can sometimes negatively impact the company. For example, spreading negative media about the company online or through other professional associations.

Bosses are behaving badly because they can. Who's stopping them? Not their bosses, not HR, and the buck stops there. They are not held accountable, nor do they suffer any consequences for poor leadership behaviors. As a result, we have hurt, abused, bad-attitude employees coming to work every day and crippling the organization from within by producing poor quality work, low quantities of labor, and spreading their done-me-wrong stories throughout the organization, affecting the optimism of others, which further fuels this vicious cycle.

Employees are afraid. They fear not being able to take care of their families if they were to lose their job. Sometimes it's because they're bad too and they're working their own bad agenda parallel to their bad boss. It could be a lack of self-confidence or insecurities, several of which could have been caused by previous poor leaders in their lives. There are things that have happened in employees' lives that also give them pause, things that may have negatively impacted their chances of getting another job (credit became poor, suffered an arrest, suspended license, lost a car, and so forth).

Bad boss behaviors must be stopped. But how do we stop bad bosses? All leaders have the potential to fail us. We are imperfect humans. To fall short is not something we're exempt from. A more fitting question to ask would be: What actions can organizations make to keep their leaders visible, consistently accountable, supported, and educated?

When people are hurt, in pain, or suffering through disappointment, it warrants immediate action, or reaction. People typically do not have enough self-control or restraint to keep hurtful events to themselves—up to retaliating. That retaliation is sometimes external against others or it's internal, causing harm or detriment to oneself (e.g., depression or anxiety attacks). Unfortunately, history has continued to repeat itself in this area.

There are thousands of blogs online on how to get your boss to respect you, give you a raise, or promote you. Thousands of books have been written on leadership. They are inspirational. They explain leadership styles in a fun, informative, or light way. I love these books; I've read hundreds of them and countless blogs outlining the same information.

However, little has been written regarding the truth, that ugly, unspoken truth about bad bosses and their dangerous tactics. You know the slimy, sticky film that lies beneath the surface of work cultures, being allowed to fester, spread, and contaminate the workplace atmosphere like termites. Nothing I've been exposed to truly uncovers the rotten apples in leadership roles that are hurting people *daily*.

They are actively working within some very prominent companies, Fortune 500 corporations, federal and government organizations, privately owned businesses, franchises, hospitals, schools, in sports, restaurants, police forces—and they are hurting people. They repeatedly abuse them with their power; they're assassinating their self-esteem, hope, the company's image, productivity, morale, and the overall integrity of service and quality leadership.

And it's time for them to stop.

But first, let's dig in to some more infamous bad boss types out there.

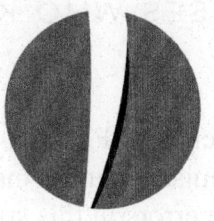

CHAPTER TWO

Thou Shalt Not Be a Know-It-All

*"The purpose of learning is growth, and our
minds, unlike our bodies, can continue growing
as we continue to live."*

—*Mortimer Adler*

We are all going to be new at something at some time in our lives. Being a novice in an area is a great thing—it means you have an opportunity to learn! As a leader, you do yourself a disservice not to pursue new information. Having a title or a group of people report to you does not somehow exempt you from the need to grow. When you learn, you add value to yourself as an individual and as a leader.

So, you've just been hired or promoted into a leadership position. Based on how you choose to proceed, you'll either become a Hero or an Outlaw. Unfortunately, most new bosses become an Outlaw, either because they don't care or they don't know any better.

A Hero will approach this new position as an opportunity to learn (grow), so he will seek out information, get to know new people, learn what isn't working, and formulate a plan to make effective change.

The Outlaw, on the other hand, will do just the opposite. Let's explore the Outlaw's most infamous wrongdoings and learn how they can cultivate a better experience for their subordinates.

In an article written by F. John Reh,[3] he accurately summarized common mistakes new managers make—I even teach some of the same errors in this style of leadership. Let's explore some of the more common mistakes of the Outlaw.

> *"As much as it may stroke your ego, to believe you know everything, YOU DON'T. You must listen to the people around you, consider their input, and keep an open mind"*
>
> —*F. J. Reh*

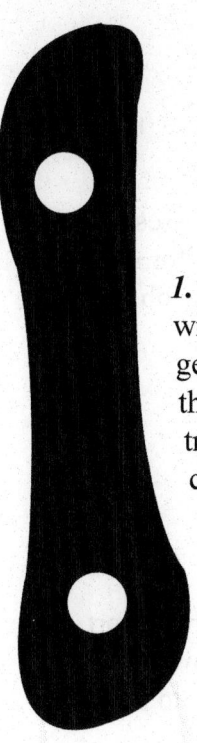

BASIC SINS OF

—THE OUTLAW—

1. Think you know everything. Think about it: a winning football team listens to their coaches; they get in the huddle and listen to their quarterback; and then in the midst of a play, they must listen to and trust each other. All winning partnerships win first at communication and trust. Be open, share, listen, and trust the people on your team.

2. Renovation rampage. You don't need to change everything as soon as you take charge. Learn what works first, and then change what doesn't.

3. Do-nothing approach. While it isn't good to immediately change everything, taking the passive approach and doing nothing isn't good either. You cannot be afraid to make smart changes. Smart, meaning, you've observed something not working, done some research, and implemented an idea to make it better.

4. Don't get to know your people. I honestly don't know how anyone expects to lead someone they haven't taken the time to get to know—doing so is pure insanity. Nonetheless, I've seen new managers commit this crime over and over again.

5. Don't stand up for your people. Pressure from work comes from many angles, and it's usually ongoing. It will always be your job as a leader to protect your people and help create an environment wherein they will be treated fairly. When you take care of others, they will take care of you.

CHARACTERISTICS

Employees who are promoted and become bad bosses are often good individual performers who were promoted for a set of skills that have little or nothing to do with their new job as a manager.

And it shows up right away.

> *"And if the blind lead the blind,*
> *both will fall into a ditch."*
> —*Matthew 15:14 (NKJV)*

Everyone knows it, starting with the employees who report to him or her. They start out clueless, knowing how to do the job of their new reports, but having no clue how to lead, motivate, or coach someone else to get the job done.

This is an old promotion process that needs to be transformed. We should pay attention to someone who successfully gets the job done on a consistent basis when seeking to promote internally, but that should not be the driving factor in giving him or her a management position. Can they lead, do they want to lead, can they have a tough conversation, and can they separate themselves from the pack? All of the aforementioned are questions that the hiring bosses need to ask themselves before the interview process begins.

Frankly, top performers should have already been challenged to complete special projects or stand in for the boss when they are unavailable. Being a candidate for promotion should never be a secret, either—they should have been groomed for the opportunity. Promoting internally is a great thing when it's done intelligently.

Internal promotions enhance the company's reputation, provide vision for employees, and promote longevity and loyalty. However, when it's done in a less-than-ethical way—

like giving the job to the buddy or the person with the highest stats—then it's quite the opposite. It is a serious wrongdoing to give someone a position of authority for any reason other than an honest and fair rationale. Whether that person be an internal or external hire, the associates find out quickly who's there for the wrong reasons and who's there for the right ones.

The Outlaw frequently thinks that what authority they have is conferred by their title; and they learn quickly that this is a myth. Their direct reports will rarely respond, and the most talented of them are the less likely to follow orders. Good bosses know they will earn their subordinates' respect and trust over time. The great leaders know their own character, competence, and follow-through in getting things done will lead to their subordinates following their lead.

TRUE STORY

I was the new boss once or twice—okay, a few times—and each time was a different experience. I was once promoted into a managerial role in an area of finance that was new to me. The management staff took a chance on my masterfully marketed ability to learn the job, because they were convinced I'd certainly be a good managerial asset.

Here I was gaining a team of people I'd never met, whose daily job functions I'd never actually done. Talk about being a new boss! I had a ninety-day plan, which consisted of getting to know the team members and learning the basics of the job. I had an introductory meeting and purchased lunch for the entire team.

It was important to me to make a true impression of my character. I'm an individual who gives 110 percent, and I needed to exemplify that by ordering gourmet stuffed baked potatoes, with sides of pasta and salad, and freshly baked cookies—not the typical pizza or subs.

When you impress someone, you have a greater chance to impact their life.

They introduced themselves and told me about their professional history and any other information they cared to share. I told them about my ninety-day plan—that I would lean on them to help me get up to speed. I told them my expectations, and then I gave them the details about who I am.

Connecting with them and caring about their needs opened the door to communication—the first step to building trust. I was alert, engaged, and amiable. I asked them to share their pain points with me about their job, and I made a promise to work on each of them.

I also had them work together to create a team mission and motto. Within the first month, all but two individuals were more relaxed, had seen my vision, and were following my lead. The two individuals who didn't stayed in their clique, and one of them had worked in this part of the finance industry so many years that she decided I didn't deserve her respect.

Yet.

So I simply practiced consistent kindness, and it created a space that allowed us to work together, even though I could tell she hadn't fully accepted me as her manager. I managed this team for nearly two years and eventually won over her buddy; she stood strong on her initial position. That was okay—I knew enough to know everyone wouldn't necessarily like me.

Don't get me wrong—my intent was not to get them to like me, but to follow the vision we all created together for our team. Hence my having them create a team mission; they would really be submitting to a standard they created. She did her job, she was an excellent average performer, and I learned along the way that no one in leadership would receive any warmth from her. It truly was her personality. No one was going to tell her what to do when she could very well be any one of our mothers.

So I followed one of the core rules I live by as a boss: make sure the employee understands their responsibilities and that they have enough information to make informed decisions and to complete their daily obligations—and then get out of their way.

When they need you, they'll seek you out.

We did share moments wherein she needed me and we formed a mutual understanding with one another. I was able to coach her buddy and propel him into a more lucrative position. This wasn't by chance. I developed the talent he already had—he was more approachable, easier to work with, and teachable.

Later, this employee reached out to me just to say thank you for valuing him and helping him become a better professional. That is what all leaders should aspire to accomplish. A simple thank-you from someone who is grateful, and became better under your leadership.

THE FIX

Most bosses learn quickly that managing is not about controlling their direct reports, or we should hope they do. New managers, who are insecure in their roles, often seek total submission to orders from their subordinates, particularly in the beginning. However, they will learn over time (if open to the lesson) that submission is not the same as commitment.

People who aren't committed won't take initiative, and if subordinates aren't taking the initiative, the manager cannot delegate effectively. The challenge for any boss is to nurture a strong sense of common commitment to shared goals—rather than one of blind allegiance to the bosses' dictates.

New bosses must focus on building a team, not creating good individual relationships. It is very common for new managers to want to work toward getting their reports to like them. When new managers focus solely on the friendly connection, they neglect a fundamental aspect of effectual leadership, wherein a leader will employ the collective power of the group to improve individual performance and dedication.

As a new boss, you will have the most impact over whether your new employees succeed or fail. After all, you control the resources they'll need, so mastering the art of negotiating for said resources should happen sooner rather than later. In parallel to that task, you should be working to establish a healthy, productive working relationship with your new employees. The key to building your working relationships is communication via multiple conversations.

In short, here are some detours for avoiding the basic sins of the new boss:

- Define your goals.

- Plan and schedule team meetings.

- Plan and schedule one-on-one meetings.

- Communicate mutual expectations early.

- Secure the resources that you and the team will need.

> *"They say that war is death's best friend, but I must offer a different point of view on that one. To me, war is like the new boss who expects the impossible. He stands over your shoulder repeating one thing, incessantly: 'Get it done, get it done.' So you work harder. You get the job done. The boss, however, does not thank you. He asks for more."*
>
> —Markus Zusak, The Book Thief

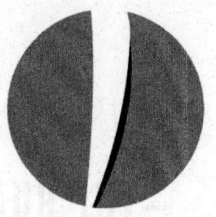

CHAPTER THREE

Thou Shalt Not Be a Bully

*"I realized that bullying never has to do with
you. It's the bully who's insecure."*

—Shay Mitchell

There isn't a single circumstance I could fathom that
would justify bullying another human being. Our forward
movement as a country in the world of technology has
unfortunately given bullies alternate platforms to play out their
antics. As a result, the definition of bullying has evolved over
the years because of the expansion of email, texting, social
media, and different virtual upgrades. Now, no one form of
bullying is worse than any other—they are all painful for the
victims of such abuse.

I personally loathe leader-to-subordinate abuse a little more
than any other type of abuse. There is something to be said of
someone who bullies those they have authority over.

There are more than likely multiple types of bullies in the
workforce. However, no matter the tactics a bully uses to abuse
its victims, it doesn't make it any less painful for those who
suffer because of it. The Workplace Bullying Institute (WBI)
completed an in-depth study and published an article on their
website outlining tactics Bully Bosses use in the workplace.[4]
WBI listed twenty-five different tactics in this article—twenty
of which are unfortunately used by people in authority within
a workplace at any give time. Falsely accusing someone of
"errors" not actually made topped the list as being used most.

Lying is the Bully's favorite tactic.

BASIC SINS OF

—THE BULLY—

1. Liar. They have to lie, because this bad boss would have to admit to being wrong. The Bully Boss is a very convincing liar and will make up anything to fit the present issue. Unfortunately, they are usually believed.

2. Reacts to criticism with denial. Denying any lack of knowledge or wrongdoing is typically the initial reaction. If their denial isn't well-received, this bad boss will shift to retaliation, playing the victim or blaming someone else.

3. Abusive and violent. The Bully Boss will treat people so badly that it causes unmatched levels of stress and fear.

4. Discriminatory. A Bully Boss may discriminate against subordinates because of their competence, popularity, achievements, status, or any other personal characteristic.

5. Lacks emotional maturity. They generally see themselves as being superior to the coworkers and as a result, this bad boss doesn't consider how their actions will affect others. They aren't even able to fathom the possibility that they could be wrong. The Bully Boss does not practice empathy.

CHARACTERISTICS

Bullies are voracious opportunists. They usually select their targets for various reasons. It may be because you're good at your job, popular with your colleagues, clients, customers; any of the aforementioned could make you a target for a Bully.

In the end, a Bully fears the exposure of his or her own inadequacy or incompetence, and your presence, competence, and popularity unwittingly agitates those fears. Being the expert to whom others come for advice, thereby gaining you more attention than the Bully, can also be a trigger. When you have a well-defined set of values, or if you're unwilling to compromise, have a strong sense of integrity, or have any type of vulnerability that can be exploited, these can make you the potential target for a Bully.

Heck, being too young, too old, too tall, too short, too skinny, too fat, too dark, too light, too poor, or too rich can all fuel aggression in a Bully. Ultimately, taking a stand for anything, especially the fair treatment of you and others, can unleash a world of jealousy within a Bully, thereby motivating them to harass you. Professional harassment is such a widespread phenomenon, and serial killer bosses who destroy people's emotional balance to fulfill their own personal goals use it.

Bullying can seriously influence an employee's perception of reality and severely damage their functionality, making it virtually impossible for them to do any work. If nothing is done to end this particular form of harassment, the end results will be catastrophic, even up to life-threatening.

There is a rampant gang mentality that is playing out within the workforce—this gang consists of bad bosses and so-called leaders. Victims of their abuse are subject to be given fewer projects, passed over for promotions, targeted as someone who can't be trusted, denied raises, unjustly fired, and emotionally or physically abused.

What people are not talking about is that these victims may also face mental health problems derived from severe stress caused by the constant bullying. Some people give up and internalize their reactions, which could lead to some form of depression. It's been an ongoing conversation among health professionals that depression can possibly lead to suicide. Suicidal thoughts can be sparked by constant experiences of bullying, being made to feel worthless, lack of appreciation for one's contributions, and lack of acknowledgment.

Bullies usually roam about the workplace spreading false rumors and information about people; and they are experts at projecting their inadequacy onto other people. Bully Bosses also think too highly of themselves, to the extent of believing they are the only ones with the correct answers.

So why are they the boss, anyway? This boss usually has had early successes in their careers that may have established something productive or lucrative. Their bad behaviors go unaddressed because of their past accomplishments. Sherri Gordon states in her article, "They [bullies] intimidate you on a regular basis, they undermine your work and impede on your successes."[5] This could not be truer. A Bully won't rest until their victim gives in or disappears.

TRUE STORY

I have worked for a Bully Boss before—three, to be exact. None of them were my direct bosses—each of them was my boss's boss. Now imagine how I felt being bullied by the boss of my boss. It was always odd for me to have that much direct negative contact with my boss's boss. The more I evaluated the experience, I concluded that this was also indicative of their bully behavior. They had no respect for my direct boss's role, skipped them in the chain of command, and opted to deal with their staff directly so they could play out their sick, serial-killing fantasies to make everyone around them feel inadequate.

Despite all the workplace bullying, one thing has never been affected: my work ethic. I always give my all at work, I take personal pride in what I do, and I am relentless about protecting my professional reputation. So when someone targets me about my work, they do so at their own risk, not having any idea of my commitment to my work ethic, follow-through, or the lengths I will travel to protect my professional character and personal reputation.

When I worked at Land Park Staffing, my direct supervisor Larry believed he was smarter than everyone else. One good thing about Larry was that he was fair; he was mean to everybody, even his boss Walter the bully! I had been with the company for two and a half years, before Walter became our department's assistant vice president.

Our company began growing quickly, and we had to expand in a hurry. Larry made manager and that left an open supervisor position, which I quickly applied for, with Larry's support. Walter the bully didn't want me to have the position, though. He kept asking if there were anyone else—he had never even met me. Everyone in my department, including my subordinates, felt I was a shoo-in. Walter made me wait an extremely long time while he searched high and low, only to circle back and have to hire me because no one else had my experience, longevity, or skill set.

Walter's bullying of me got so bad over the next two and a half years that I started keeping a work journal. I am a navy veteran so discipline is not something I lack, but under this man's leadership, I was written up for the first time *in my life*, on the grounds of "being combative," which confused me. My work was impeccable, I came to work early each day (even as a salaried employee), and I never called in sick. So being combative when discussing new processes must have been the only angle he could come up with, and unfortunately, Human Resources backed him up on it.

This is an example of why most HR organizations cannot be trusted; they do not operate in fairness, which is another book in itself. Now I later learned that being combative is an example of a potential attitude issue, and when a leader uses the word *attitude* to deliver disciplinary action, it is important to provide an example how said behavior is having a negative effect on a person's job performance. I didn't know this at the time of the incident, so I just signed the write-up out of *fear* that I may lose my job if I didn't comply with this abuse. This was crystal-clear proof that I wasn't dealing with a work-related issue; this boss didn't like me personally, for reasons I may never know.

Looking back, I wish I had known how to stand up for myself or challenge the write-up in a way that would've created a growth opportunity for him, myself, and HR so that we all could've learned from this situation.

I was doing everything I could to post out to a different department (boss) or even leave the company because I was so upset and emotional every day after interacting with Walter. I must make it clear: I'm not an emotional person; my tolerance level far exceeds that of the average adult, so trust me when I tell you I was being severely bullied. It wasn't easy to leave. I know now that's because there was something I was supposed to learn there, which I'm sharing with you throughout this book. I needed to pass the life test of practicing undeserved submission in addition to underserved kindness, and mostly the leadership responsibility of protecting my staff from bullies like Walter. I was able to coach them, give recommendations to them, and guide them into other jobs. I singlehandedly did that with each one of my staff members who had the courage to leave—before I was laid off.

It is absolutely no fun to be bullied, and it's extremely painful to be bullied by someone Monday through Friday of every week. You feel completely helpless; you need your job to take care of your family so you can't walk out like you dream of doing every night. You just have to endure it until another opportunity opens up for you.

This awful boss Walter would make me come in on Saturdays to supervise other managers' staff, and he would clock my breaks and lunches to the minute. He would constantly make sarcastic remarks about my hair, my divorce, my team, my work shift—you name it. Anything he could quickly make a joke about at my expense, he would.

Leadership is a choice. When you assume a position of authority, you make the choice to lead. Management is the discipline of getting things done right. Leadership is also the art of doing what is right for the good of the organization and its people; management is executing that goal. Leadership should inspire everyone in its path, not tear them down. Inspiration materializes from purpose, knowing what you do and why you do it.

Bullying has never materialized into something great. When I left Land Park Staffing, they had to pay me via a five-year severance package. God protected me while there and blessed me on my way out the door. Walter tried his best to fire me, more than once too; but ultimately, the best he could do was ensure I was included on the first round of company layoffs.

Four years later, I ended up back at this same company in a different position (training). Corporate America is a fickle, dog-eat-dog world, with large downsizings and frequent mass hirings. The previous company (Land Park Staffing) was bought out by a new CEO and changed their name due to the awful reputation it had gained in its business affairs. The new owners demoted and fired all of the existing leadership and started over with a new focus and business model. Walter had been demoted, and now sits in a cubicle the size of my old one.

"A great person attracts great people and knows how to hold them together."

—*Johann Wolfgang von Goethe*

THE FIX

The tough times we go through in our life will show us more about who we are if we pay attention. I learned about my challenge areas, my strengths, and my purpose because of these experiences. So I'm not sharing my experiences to gain pity or remorse—I'm sharing because it is my story, and because I hope anyone who can relate to this will see that they too can grow up from this pain.

I read a meme once that said, "Pain changes you." I became intoxicated from the truth packed in those three words. Immediately, several painful experiences flashed through my memory and in hindsight, I could see the change so clearly. I now saw things and people differently because of pain. I spoke differently, and I responded to situations differently. Pain had diminished my level of faith, it had doused my confidence, and to my own disgust, it had actually made me weak.

Most people will tell you, "If it doesn't kill you, it will make you stronger." But does it really? Is it considered strong to become paranoid, judgmental, guarded, and emotionally detached? I don't think so. I think you simply develop coping mechanisms for protecting your new wounds out of fear of ever feeling that pain again. There is no strength in fear; the strength is in defeating fear.

If you are a Bully Boss, therapy to discover the root cause of your bully behaviors is paramount. Then get connected with an organization that has a culture of mutual respect and accountability. Tackling bully behavior isn't an overnight fix, but I believe if the intent to do better exists, you'll become better over time.

If you're an employee who is being bullied:

- Keep records of all encounters with your Bully Boss.

- Be prepared for retaliation (be your best in every area, attendance, job performance, etc.).

- Refresh your résumé and cover letter, and start searching for a new job.

- While you're there, learn your lesson from this (who you are, your passions and growth opportunities).

If you're a bully boss:

- Own your character flaws.

- Get therapy. Many job medical benefits offer assistance for the cost.

- Recruit an accountability partner, another leader you can trust to tell you the truth about your behaviors.

- Seek out leadership seminars and books—you'll need new information to transform into a new you.

"Great leaders don't set out to be a leader . . . they set out to make a difference. It's never about the role—always about the goal."

—*Lisa Haisha*

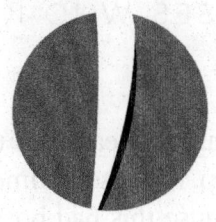

CHAPTER FOUR

Thou Shalt Not Be Ignorant

"When too many people, either ignorantly or intentionally, but happily going in the wrong direction; anyone with a positive reflection and good intention goading them to do introspection for the course correction or right selection of the partner is most likely to be branded by a few of most of them to be a negative person."

—*Anuj Somany*

Have you ever been involved in a project with someone who had no idea what was going on? Or how about when you're teamed with someone who acts like they do know what's going on, but the rest of you know they don't? Neither of those scenarios is the easiest to work through, and I've experienced them both.

In the first scenario, one typically becomes frustrated because they know this means they'll be doing double their share of the work. When a clueless person acts like they know what they're doing out of fear of being judged or exposed, then everyone else involved in said project has to pacify their ignorance while simultaneously getting the project completed per expectations. The upside: you have some type of control of the final outcome and what gets turned in from your collective group project.

When you report to a Clueless Boss, it gets a little more difficult to shine, because the leader represents the group. The boss is the boss, we obligatorily follow, and when they don't know what they're doing, it speaks for the group. If someone from the group speaks up, it can sometimes look like they're the bad guy, especially because this bad boss is typically regarded by most people as a nice person.

Now, we're going to learn more about the Clueless Boss and how to deal with him.

—CLUELESS BOSS—

1. Remains clueless. You may have been given a leadership opportunity because of who you know or the type of degree you have, but to remain clueless once in a leadership role is criminal indeed.

2. Refuses to make decisions. Some bad boss types who are incompetent refuse to make any decisions at all, or make ones without researching; either way, it leads to chaos in the workplace. This lack of courage can lead to dissension.

3. Fails to provide clear direction. It proves true that it's a little difficult to provide clear direction when you don't know what direction to go. This is a sin that happens as a result of this bad boss not taking initiative to learn the things they don't know.

4. Trying to become friends with employees who report to you. This bad boss does this in hopes of gaining a "shadow boss"—a Clueless Boss who will casually bring up work issues so that they can use their responses or ideas. Not to mention the conflict of interest of developing such a relationship with a subordinate.

5. Dishonest. Generally, a Clueless Boss's dishonesty is reactionary. Reactionary because remaining ignorant in a leadership position will always put you in a situation to lie about what you have or haven't done, do or do not know, both to your superiors and your subordinates.

CHARACTERISTICS

The unskilled boss is all too popular; if leadership were a country, the Clueless Bosses would be the majority. So many bosses fail when it comes to staying abreast of how things work. No, I don't believe they need to be the best at the actual job in order to know how to get the job done. The other layer that contributes to this being a majority is the age-old hiring of unqualified acquaintances at leadership level, or promoting someone just because of their tenure, and so forth. They fail at getting to know the people they work with, which further fuels their ignorance. This serial-killing boss will throw his or her own subordinates under the bus at any moment. They lack loyalty, compassion, and connectivity. They are reactive and not proactive, and they are also habitual liars.

The Clueless Boss lies, because they refuse to learn and ask questions. It's more important in their minds that they appear to know what's going on as opposed to actually learning what's going on.

Now it's rare for someone to be promoted who has absolutely no skills. She may be awesome at task A and maybe even task B, but sucks at task C—task C being the actual job function she currently manages. This serial killer has been known to be a friend of a friend, an undercover friend, a distant family member, a lover, or a mistress of someone high up.

It's very unheard of for a clueless, degree- or non-degree-having, skill-less person to be hired to lead people without there being some underlying connections. Now, there are times when executive management wants to shake things up by bringing in a fresh face or someone new to lead the pack to new levels of success, but typically this person isn't completely clueless on the processes of the job at hand. When I talk about the Clueless Boss, I'm referring to the one who has no idea what their people do, what the job entails, how to lead, or how to do anything that would sustain or improve the current job process.

This serial killer boss is insecure and cowardly—those are the only explanations for someone stepping into a role as a leader clueless and then remaining clueless their entire tenure as boss—with zero motivation to learn what their people do. This boss is known for pretending, and they talk a good game but have absolutely no ability to make winning plays. The Clueless Boss is really a follower who lacks innovation, is a heavy delegator, doesn't know the job at all, takes credit for other's ideas, and repeats what you say. Beware of these dangerous behaviors.

The Clueless Boss also lacks communication skills, so it's no wonder they cannot communicate to you what they don't know. As their employee, you're usually malnourished, neglected, and pretty darn clueless as well. You need feedback, deadlines, and communication before and during projects.

Most gurus have written books on how we should manage up and be proactive so we can get the things we need from this serial-killing boss. These leadership experts tell us to set our own meetings, ask the boss what their priorities are, what needs to be done, keep notes, save e-mails, and keep good records of all you do and all the conversations you have so that you can *defend* yourself if your work ever comes in to question.

I find it a little unfair that of all the *experts* and their collective knowledge, this is the only option explored. It is a jaw-dropping thought that a lazy, incompetent boss can report to work every day, never learn their job, and potentially lead a department or organization right into the crapper, while the subordinates stand by and document it. All of us have to come together to explore other possibilities. Where is the Clueless Boss's boss, and how can we motivate them to hold this bad boss accountable? What can we do to ensure someone who reports to this bad boss doesn't unfairly lose their job, or be forced to leave a job they love because of the antics of the Clueless Boss?

How about we train up the lazy bosses or fire them? No, instead, these experts figured out a way to provide zero accountability for the boss. What does it take for everyone to see this does not work, that we must break out of this awful habit? Coping tools are completely necessary. There is a time and place for everything. Even I had to cope for a while at Land Park Staffing. But as a leadership guru, the coping tools should be the blog, while reforming the boss should be the book.

TRUE STORY

I was a new employee at a new company and received zero training on my job duties. Sure, I had worked similar jobs in my previous professional history, but I had never worked for this company. I had no idea what the culture, dress code, or business ethics were for this organization. My first six weeks on the job, I sat at my desk and twiddled my thumbs. Several times I would ask my boss for work, and each time she would send me to someone who would have no idea why I was even talking to them.

To show up every day, ready and motivated to get something done, and to be given zero direction is the ultimate torture. The longer I was there, the more I understood what was happening.

She could not teach me what she didn't know.

I learned this serial killer boss had been with the company for years in a different capacity, was new to the management role in this department, had been in her current role (as my boss) for ten months, but *still* didn't know a thing about what the department did. Zero effort was done on her part to ensure she was up to par, and apparently, her boss hadn't done her due diligence to ensure her new manager was up to par either.

I had been on this job almost two months when my boss's boss (Mary) called me with a request. Apparently, I was next in the chain of command when my boss was out of the office (something I didn't know), and she requested something simple, but I wasn't equipped to carry it out.

After completely making a fool of myself in front of our client due to my lack of information, I called Mary directly. I apologized for my ignorance. She asked me a few simple questions and learned that I didn't have the software or the supplies I needed to properly adhere to her request. She apologized to me and said the incident exposed some holes that she would make sure were filled.

Mary called me each day during my boss's vacation to check in on me and send me things I needed to carry out tasks she wanted to give me.

When my boss returned, she was apparently heavily reprimanded for what had been exposed while she was out, and she made sure I knew she was angry with me. She unapproved a vacation day she had approved the first day I started. She made me retake two software exams I had already passed on my own a month earlier, saying I needed to score higher to prove my competence. She started sending me on goose chases around the office and began making very sarcastic comments like, "Maybe you should tell Mary what you learned today," or "Do you have what you need to do your job today?"

A bully at her finest.

Because she hadn't been managed or trained appropriately, she had no pause about behaving badly and seeking revenge when her shortcomings as a leader were exposed. All the way around, there was no respect for the company, their clients, or the overall culture. These were a group of people who weren't exposed to vision and purpose; expectations and consequences had not been properly communicated. They made the age-old mistake from the very top all the way down: people were thrown into or hand-selected into roles and given a bottom line with no instructions on how to get there.

*"It is absurd that a man should rule others,
who cannot rule himself."*

—Latin Proverb

INTERVIEW RECAP WITH ANTHONY: BEST/WORSE BOSS INTERVIEW SARAH VS. TRACY

Best: Sarah had an open-door policy at her real estate office. Her expectations were clear. She was firm but fair. Sarah was real—very relatable but never crossed the line. She was a nice person and taught us to use the chain of command by bringing issues to her first. She enforced the rules, and we always felt respected. She promoted people quickly and frequently, and she knew how to make a decision.

Worse: At the tax office, Tracy *didn't know how* to separate her business from her personal life. She didn't make her objectives or expectations clear. There were no work goals. She *never* knew how to fill out the workday for her employees. Tracy was very unprofessional and unpolished. She seemed to be knowledgeable of some things but could not articulate her ideas or knowledge effectively. I had lots of downtime at work and had no idea what else could be done. Working for Tracy made me feel like I was always behind the eight ball. The experience of working for a Clueless Boss stifled my advancement opportunities and chipped away at my job confidence.

THE FIX

Business owners and executive management: it is never okay to hire Mr./Ms. Clueless to lead your staff. If you absolutely must hire someone who knows nothing about the job at hand, then you must equip them with a learning plan and timeline to commit to, request follow-through on those milestones, and provide a subject matter expert as a point of contact for your new boss until they gain their footing.

A manager once suggested to me that one way to deal with a Clueless Boss was to "talk to your boss and offer additional help where they are weakest." Here is my concern with this advice: it doesn't guarantee a win for the subordinate. Will this boss appreciate or recognize this subordinate in action and deeds, comp time off, a raise, or a promotion? No. Will this serial killer support them behind closed doors, stand up for them, speak well of them out of their presence? I doubt it.

Helping them could essentially make you a target, especially if this Clueless Boss becomes fearful that you can take their spot. Even worse, you could end up doing their job and yours, with zero recognition and zero financial reward. There are just too many variables to this method that could go wrong for the subordinate. To which this manager's reply was for me to simply "draw clear lines between your workload and the boss's" or just find another job if neither of the aforementioned approaches work.

I say document, document, and document. As soon as you realize you're in this position, start documenting and follow up on all conversations where this boss is requesting your assistance or input on the job in e-mail. Print and save these e-mails for your records—do not forward them to an outside e-mail address.

Simultaneously, you should be using your evenings making sure your résumé is up-to-date and start searching for new job opportunities, whether internally or externally. Create options for yourself, and do so with urgency. Employees are in charge of their careers and don't have to subject themselves to jobs and bosses who refuse to build a quality team of professionals around them.

Every employee has the right to work in a place where they will grow in responsibility, financially, professionally, and in character. If you can find poor leadership within any organization, rest assured you'll also find unfair compensation, discrimination, frustrated workers, and poor quality among other career dream-killers. What really sucks about this outcome is that today we live in an Information Age where bad news travels instantly, thereby allowing competitors to profit from your organization's lack of leadership.

Clueless Bosses lack vision, skill, and interpersonal communication skills. You can always spot this serial killer in a meeting or during any sort of team interaction or in the face of any conflict, because they lack the confidence to speak up, resolve, or improve anything. They'll be the one not talking, or they will show up talking a whole lot, but saying nothing of substance.

The actions they do take typically have a negative outcome; their very presence and lack of knowledge encourages dishonesty, fuels gossip, and destroys the overall camaraderie of their team or department. When leaders lack the competency to manage his or her team, productivity drops, morale diminishes, and ultimately the company fails.

The ugly truth is the Clueless Boss has and will always exist; the upside is there will always be a need for what I supply: innovative, introspective training that transforms leadership for the better, which enhances employee work ethic. The downside is people may get hurt, abused, and unfairly treated in the interim.

I heard Iyanla Vanzant say once during a life class show on the OWN Network that, "All things are lessons God will have us learn." I believe people really do enter our lives to teach us something, as life lessons are extremely valuable and shouldn't be overlooked or taken for granted. If you're ever subjected to this serial killer, although extremely frustrating and annoying, there are several gold nuggets amidst the trials, things of value that you can learn, which could one day make you a better leader yourself.

In short, here are some detours for avoiding the basic sins of the Clueless Boss:

- **Listen.** Information is always being shared within the workspace, so be present and pay attention when more experienced people are talking.

- **Take notes.** Don't rely on your memory. It is perfectly fine to take notes so you have a reference point for information you will most likely need again.

- **Ask questions.** Don't allow pride or fear of judgment to leave you in the dark. When you don't know something, ask—and ask until the answer has been proven effective.

- **Build rapport.** Get to know your coworkers, especially those who are veterans within the company, and learn from them.

"A competent leader can get efficient service from poor troops, while on the contrary an incapable leader can demoralize the best of troops."

—John J. Pershing

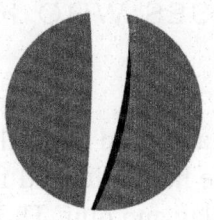

CHAPTER FIVE

Thou Shalt Not Be Lazy

*"A person is being lazy if he is able
to carry out some activity that he ought to
carry out, but is disinclined to do so
because of the effort involved."*

—*Neel Burton*

To lead a person or group of people in the successful completion of any task, it requires effort. Yes, sometimes that effort will take you out of your comfort zone. For example, exerting some effort won't always afford you the luxury of remaining silent when your people need you to speak up.

Neel Burton explains in his article for Psychology Today, "He (a person) is being lazy if his motivation to spare himself effort trumps his motivation to do the right thing or the expected thing."[6] Each of us has the power to choose. We can choose to do the right thing or the wrong thing in any situation. Laziness is a choice.

Certainly the circumstances and consequences surrounding each choice can sometimes make us feel like our choice is sabotaged, but we always have the power to choose. I had a boss who was once directed to let go of several people from his department because of a chain email joke that was passed around between them, but he felt strongly that the punishment didn't fit the crime. He knew the character of his people, and most of them were his top performers. However, he decided to do as he was told. He sat next to an HR representative in a small conference room and fired over fifty people. He couldn't sleep that night, because he felt he had failed as a leader, so he came to work the next day and quit. Though the choice to fight for his employees' jobs had gone, he made the choice to no longer work for a company whose ethics he didn't share.

You can do nothing, or you can do something—the choice is yours. Own your power to choose, act on it, and do something today that you can be proud of tomorrow.

> *"Laziness drives away talent, leaving the company with workers who are limited in their capabilities or held back by the systems of behavior that is ingrained in the company's culture."*
>
> *—Stephen C. Harper*

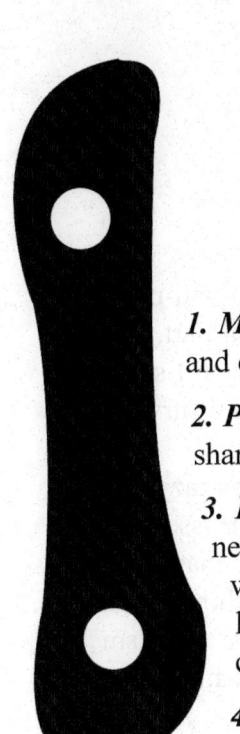

BASIC SINS OF

—THE LAZY BOSS—

1. MIA. They are missing in action. Unpunctual, slow, and out of the loop.

2. Poor communicators. Waiting for the Lazy Boss to share updates will always leave others in the dark.

3. Play the blame game. When things go wrong, it's never their fault. Because they have been disengaged, when it's time to explain a shortcoming, their only line of defense is to blame their team or other coworkers.

4. Unethical. Let's face it—you can't be lazy and honest. If you're not doing the work, someone else is. So when the Lazy Boss's manager asks them for updates, or their employees ask them for direction, they are not prepared with facts and truth, because they haven't done the work to know the answers.

5. You don't think through your choices. Because decisions are generally ignored until they are due (because you've been too lazy to care), you cannot research and analyze what is best to do. So most decisions are based on instinct or hearsay.

CHARACTERISTICS

You usually don't hear from this serial killer boss until something is wrong. They tend to have a cut-and-paste mentality because it requires very little effort on their part. The Lazy Boss won't help staff when volume is high, won't stand up for their staff when needed, and often lie, which is a survival tactic so their lack of work isn't exposed.

Don't get me wrong. It does take some effort to be lazy, but not as much effort as it takes to be productive. Lazy Bosses and bosses who don't really want the responsibility of managing people try to take shortcuts. If they don't like something about you or your work, rather than give you constructive criticism to help you develop, they'll start attacking you with vague generalities—like your attitude or teamwork attributes.

Do not get sucked in by this. Attitude is a label for behavior that could honestly represent anything, and no one can see labels. There has to be an example of observable bad behavior any time your boss is making an attempt to coach you up.

The Lazy Boss gives the least possible guidance to subordinates, and they try to achieve control through less obvious means. They generally believe that people excel when they are left alone to respond to their responsibilities and obligations in their own ways. This boss expects their subordinates to solve problems on their own, and it is a wide hit-or-miss with whether or not the subordinates were given the tools or resources they need to solve problems or perform their job duties. This boss personality congenitally implies a complete hands-off approach.

The Lazy Boss is dangerous in situations where group members lack the knowledge or experience they need to complete tasks and make decisions. Some people are not good at setting their own deadlines, managing projects, or solving problems on their own. In such situations, projects usually go off track and deadlines are missed because team members did not get enough guidance or feedback from their leaders.

Not only do lazy leaders negatively affect their subordinates, but their actions (or lack thereof) also run through the entire organization right down to the bottom line. Therefore, it's vital to deal with laziness as soon as possible to avoid infecting your company's culture and performance.

By dealing with laziness upfront, you avoid allowing it to permeate your entire company. The Lazy Boss could slant other employees' perceptions about an organization's expectations. When this bad boss is consistently absent (physically or mentally) from meetings, projects, or deadlines, it could very well send the message to his coworkers that the company accepts this type of behavior.

Laziness particularly affects newer employees who are learning by example of what's acceptable in their new environment. A lazy worker lowers the bar for fresh talent, severely tainting the culture and creating a foundation of laziness for future contributors.

If the Lazy Boss's lack of effort continues to go unnoticed and unaddressed, this can cause tension between the subordinates and their boss. Hard workers can tell when their boss isn't involved in the day-to-day work process. Being a lazy, serial-killing boss is one of the worst types of murders one could commit. For the employee who steps up and assumes a management role and then does little to nothing in their leadership role, they become universally despised. This would easily be a felony crime in the context of this book. The subordinates who are responsible for picking up the slack are resentful and unhappy. Nothing makes a work environment more loathsome than a slacker boss.

When this type of dysfunction exists in a company's culture, employees feel powerless to change this dysfunction, so the good ones leave to find employment elsewhere.

TRUE STORY

If awards were given for being lazy, my boss Jane would walk the red carpet all the way to claim her prize. Well, maybe not actually *get it herself*. She might summon someone else to get it for her.

What made her laziness so obvious were the multiple teams that shared the same area of the office. Other bosses would walk through and say good morning, and facilitate quick huddles to share the day's expectations. On any given day, you could find one of Jane's employees asking another employee for an update on what's happening, because we certainly weren't getting communication from her. You would only hear from her if there were a problem.

One day, she walked around to tell everyone that some executives would be visiting the building and we needed to be on our best behavior.

Once, she made it to my desk to share the message, "Oh, I don't have to worry about you. You're really quiet." My neighbor looked at me with a cocked eyebrow. We chatted all the time among ourselves! Thankfully, during the time I reported to Jane, I knew my job pretty well. I had worked with several of the other associates in the past, so I did some self-initiated sidebar chats to learn specifics about how this company interpreted several guidelines, and I was pretty much solid after that.

Apparently, word got around that I knew what I was doing, and there were two people on my team struggling. They were clueless, and complaints were pouring in on their lack of know-how. So for the second time ever, Jane actually talked to me and said, "The other managers were telling me how great a job you've been doing, and I want to know if you'd mind training two of your teammates who are struggling."

Imagine my internal distain for her statement—other managers were telling her how great I was doing. You haven't said anything of substance to me since I started, and now you want me to risk my own workload falling behind so I can train employees you never trained?

Of course I said, "Sure, no problem." I wasn't altogether positive if it's ever a good idea to say no to your boss; she may not talk to me, but she's still the person who will be completing my annual review, so I agreed to help.

Each of these individuals sat with me for three full days, a total of six days of training for me. I sent my boss a summary of my observation of their attentiveness, comprehension, and projection of how they'll do going forward. I got an e-mail reply that simply said, "Thank you."

That is when I learned I had a passion for training, so I was hired for a training position after only six months, although the rules state you have to work in each role one full year. Jane's boss had been observing me and signed off on my early departure. There is always something to learn or gain—even from a bad boss.

> *"Lazy people tend not to take chances, but express*
> *themselves by tearing down other's work."*
>
> —*Ann Rule*

THE FIX

First, find out what is the cause of this individual's lazy behavior. Laziness is sometimes rooted in a lack of self-discipline, the need for recognition, lack of emotional support, or a lack of self-efficacy.

As executive leaders of these bosses, you'll need to adopt methods for motivating your Lazy Bosses, making them accountable to goal-setting and follow-through, and maybe even implementing a reward system for the completion of tasks and meeting goals. More importantly, have a frank discussion with this Lazy Boss about his or her underperformance, being sure to clarify other (outside) issues that may be causing their laziness. Be open to new ways to help this boss improve. It could be a much-needed vacation, switching their shift to a 4/10, or providing a longer lunch. As I mentioned, if you value them, you must be willing to flex and create an environment wherein they can improve and thrive.

There are circumstances wherein a Lazy Boss can go undetected, like when their followers are highly skilled, well-informed, have pride in their work, and possess the drive to perform exceptionally on their own. Also, when their employees happen to be trustworthy and highly experienced. The Lazy Boss is never a good idea when employees feel a sense of insecurity at the unavailability of their boss or when the leader will not or cannot provide their employees with regular feedback. Everyone must be accountable to making sure we have quality leaders in place within every organization and on each team represented within every company.

Accountability doesn't come cheap. It takes effort, time, and money, but it's all worth it. Invest in the training, make time to check in, follow up, and make time to get to know those who labor among you.

As a leader, we need to know what literature has to say, to the appropriate, specific characteristics of our unique leadership style, so we can become the best leaders possible. Good leadership enhances the environment, increases production and output, develops high morale among staff, and minimizes problems that happen in the course of doing business, thereby saving the company money. Bad habits, just like good habits, will become ingrained in workplace behaviors and produce results, be they good or bad.

In short, here are some things you can do to avoid Lazy Boss behaviors:

- **Check in.** Meet with your team regularly—ask them what they need.

- **Make a to-do list.** Once you've created this list, add a timeline to it.

- **Build an accountability group.** Set up consistent meeting times with other leaders in your department to check in and make sure you are up to par.

"Leaders aren't born. They are made. And they are made just like anything else, through hard work. And that's the price we'll have to pay to achieve that goal, or any goal."

—*Vince Lombardi*

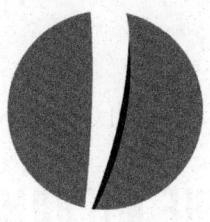

CHAPTER SIX

Thou Shalt Not Suffocate a Subordinate

"A leader is best when people barely know he exists, when his work is done, his aim fulfilled, they will say: we did it ourselves."

—*Lao Tzu*

The Micromanager is probably the most infamous of all the bad bosses. Their habits are vivid, all too common, and leave no one exempt. A CEO can be micromanaged by her investors. A manager can be micromanaged by his boss. An employee could even micromanage another employee. This killer is highly contagious and extremely dangerous. They have a bag of excuses for such torture that can sound pretty convincing to the untrained ear.

The reality is they suffocate and they know it and they tend to believe it's a necessary evil.

The most frequent motivations for micromanagement are emotional insecurity, doubts regarding employees' competence, or addiction to specific order. They are generally internal and related to the personality of the manager. However, external factors—such as severe or increased time or performance pressure, instability of managerial position, organizational culture, and unrealistic goals—can also play a role in the severity of the micromanaging style of this boss.

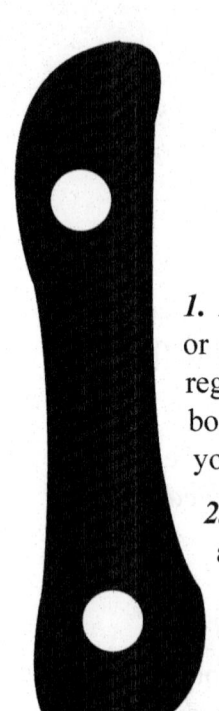

BASIC SINS OF

—THE MICROMANAGER—

1. Monitoring too closely. Bosses who physically or virtually check in with you throughout the day regarding status updates. This is also revealed by bosses who request end-of-day/week recaps of what you've accomplished.

2. Intervening too much. You can see this one in a leader when they want to proofread everything before submission or altogether overstep you and do the job themselves.

3. Setting too many priorities simultaneously. Everything is urgent with this bad boss. They'll give you five projects all with the same due date and expect high quality on each one.

4. Discussing things to death. Meeting after meeting after meeting followed by follow-up emails about the meeting, onward to setting a new meeting about following up.

5. Suffocating employees, thereby hindering their growth. This is the primary lethal behavior of the Micromanager. They won't let up, won't give you space, and demand complete control. What is there left for an employee to do when a boss doesn't give them an opportunity to do anything?

CHARACTERISTICS

The Micromanager murders people one by one with their sickening, overbearing tactics and are infamously known for not even knowing what it takes for the job to get done. This bad boss kills by suffocating you. A Micromanager will stay on top of you until you pass out, die, or become obsolete. They refuse to let up. You will either die voluntarily by leaving the situation or you'll die a miserable, emotional, ambitionless death wherein you show up and function in a robotic manner, no longer concerned with the quality or quantity of your work, inner-office relationships, or appearance.

Micromanagement is a management style whereby a manager closely observes or controls the work of subordinates; it generally has a negative connotation, which I believe is fitting. The Micromanager can be extended to any social context wherein a person exhibits an inability to be flexible. Any time a boss is obsessing with the minutest of details, it causes a direct management failure in the ability to focus on the major details.

These boss types are usually irritated when a subordinate makes decisions without consulting them, even if the decisions are within the subordinate's level of authority. Micromanaging also frequently involves requests for unnecessary and overly detailed reports (*Report-a-citis Disease*, I call it). This bad boss tends to require constant and detailed performance feedback of every worker that reports to him or her. He takes employees' attention away from doing the very work they're being micromanaged to complete. This type of leadership clouds overall goals, but this serial killer will accept that potential inefficiency as a minor consequence in comparison to their need to control everything around them.

Although micromanagement is often easily recognized by employees, Micromanagers rarely view themselves as such. We all know denial is a known trait found in addictive behavior.

Micromanagers will often rebut allegations of their stalking antics by offering a more liquefied language to characterize their management style, such as "structured," or "hands-on." This serial killer has the tendency to even perform the duties of their subordinates. Other times, they'll tell their employees what to do, then dictate that the job be done a certain way, regardless of whether that way is the most effective or efficient one.

Micromanagement is a tactic consciously chosen for the purpose of eliminating unwanted employees. The serial killer sets unreachable standards that he or she then invokes as grounds for termination of those employees; these standards could be either specific to certain employees or generally applicable but selectively enforced only against particular employees. They will also attempt this same pressure by other means in an effort to create a stressful workplace in which the undesired employees no longer desire to participate. When this stress becomes so severe and pervasive, the employees will most likely quit.

TRUE STORY

Remember Larry? Now, Larry's *boss* Walter was a bully, but Larry was a Micromanager. Even before Walter became his boss, Larry would micromanage his team.

As Larry's team lead, I became privy to what a serial killer of this magnitude can do to people. In our department, the team lead acted as a motivator, trainer, and messenger for the subordinates. My job was to be their first point of contact. I also would pull and sort the reports that Larry would have to turn in at the end of the day to his boss.

Larry was extremely involved with the staff—or *hands-on*. He would walk around most of the day, checking their monitors, stopping by to confront them of their previous days' mistakes for anyone who showed up on the naughty report. Sometimes he would even pull them into an impromptu conference room for a quick conversation regarding their performance.

I knew right away, as his team lead, I had to be the complete opposite of him in order to bring balance. So I made sure to be approachable—a listener and a coach. These people would come to me with questions that were really disguised for them to vent about how crazy Larry was making them. I felt like more of a counselor than anything during this time. I was always talking someone off the ledge, out of quitting, and helping them learn things they could do to hopefully make their encounters with Larry shorter or less formal. Essentially, you would need to manage yourself first.

Unfortunately, everyone isn't as organized or into the details so this isn't an easy thing to teach.

Regardless of a Micromanager's motive, the effects can be lethal. The behaviors of this serial killer create resentment in manager-subordinate and subordinate-subordinate relationships. Micromanagers damage trust, zap employee confidence, and cultivate an all-around poor working atmosphere. The habits of a Micromanager suggest to employees that a manager does not trust their work or judgment. It is a major factor in triggering employee disengagement, often to the point of promoting a dysfunctional work environment wherein the leadership hierarchy as a whole is labeled as control freaks, as opposed to knowledgeable managers who can be trusted.

"So much of what we call management consists
of making it difficult for people to work."

—*Peter Drucker*

THE FIX

Severe forms of micromanagement can stifle opportunities for the learning and development of interpersonal skills, completely eliminate trust, and even provoke anti-social behavior. They also often rely on inducing fear in the employees to achieve more control, which can severely affect the self-esteem of employees as well as their mental and physical health.

As leaders, we have to ask ourselves: is there anything, any quota, any goal, and any task worth us putting the mental and physical health of our employees at risk? Is there? Sure, most jobs come with a certain level of stress—that's just it: most jobs. We don't need the added stress of poor leadership by micromanaging serial killers.

The most detrimental effects of micromanagement can extend beyond the walls of a company, specifically when the behavior of these bad bosses becomes severe enough to force out skilled employees who are valuable to competitors. Some employees may complain about their Micromanager in social settings or to friends and colleagues who are affiliated with other firms in a field. Outside observers may even notice these issues and decide to talk about it with other people they may know.

We all know the power of word-of-mouth. It's unstoppable. It just travels and travels, and it gets worse the farther it travels. Ultimately, this damages a company's reputation, which then feeds the insecurity among management within the company, thereby prompting further micromanaging antics among managers who use it to cope with their insecurities, perpetuating a vicious cycle. Who's going to set a new standard? Who has the bravery to innovate a new standard? When will this type of murder stop?

Here are some guidelines to follow:

- **Be transparent.** If you are a Micromanager, let your people know you know that. Assure them you're working on it and that your intentions are positive.

- **Fall back.** You have to give your people an opportunity to perform. If they miss the mark, you get the opportunity to coach them up.

- **Don't be afraid to let your employees fail.** Learning from mistakes builds confidence, develops maturity, and reveals an individual's level of commitment to their job.

- **For day-to-day management,** define performance metrics based on core priorities and measure those only, ignoring everything else. Save the other stuff for your monthly one-on-one meeting.

- **Recognize and reward.** When someone does something right, smart, or good, let them know. Share it with the team and find some way to reward them.

"The best executive is the one who has sense enough to pick good men to do what he wants done, and self-restraint enough to keep from meddling with them while they do it."

—*Theodore Roosevelt*

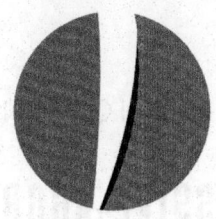

CHAPTER SEVEN

Thou Shalt Not Create Chaos

*"The battlefield is a scene of constant chaos.
The winner will be the one who controls the
chaos, both his own and the enemies."*

—*Napoleon Bonaparte*

This boss type was by far one of the more interesting personalities to research. It may be because of the twists and turns that happen under this leadership style, or it could be because I've seen this boss figure in action more times than I care to remember.

These tactics sometimes get confused within the authority aura that higher-ups exude. When you really see the behaviors of this serial killer for what they are, your own intuition will tell you to watch out, and you won't be surprised by their backstabbing, dirty tricks.

The Passive-Aggressive Boss generally is known as a high-energy, get-things-done type of person, all the while driving everyone around them crazy with their nutty behavior. I've come to realize that any boss who continues in bad behavior for long periods deserves your sympathy more than anything. They are struggling and don't have any idea how they can improve, or sadly that they need to.

—THE PASSIVE-AGGRESSIVE BOSS—

1. Indecisive. Constantly changes their mind about what should be done and how (any boss who changes their mind all the time will send any employee to the loony bin).

2. Lacks integrity. Boss takes full credit of the team's work (this sabotages employee recognition/ advancement opportunities and diminishes morale).

3. Untrustworthy. Exploiting an employee's talent, which abuses the employee's trust.

4. Manipulative. Boss purposefully restricts information the worker needs to do a good job, preventing workers from producing their best work.

5. Insecure. Criticizes an employee in public, thereby tearing away at their confidence.

6. Selfish. Makes everything about themselves; cunningly changes the subject back to themselves, no matter the situation.

CHARACTERISTICS

Passive-aggressive behaviors that exist in bosses may be more of a problem than when exhibited in employees. These behaviors in bosses are typically much more prevalent than companies would be willing to admit. Passive-Aggressive Bosses make life in the workplace very difficult for their employees, by making it challenging and stressful to the point of exhaustion. This serial killer can destroy the morale of their employees over and over again, like taking the knife out and putting it back in. They demoralize their subordinates, causing them to work less, produce less, and eventually care less, which leads to decreased work output, poor quality, and a waste of money for the company.

Ever had a boss describe himself as a nice person who doesn't like conflict? They hide behind this hideous façade, all the while stirring up conflict between everyone in reach. Ever worked for someone who sent you constant mixed signals, seemed as if they liked you one minute, and then it felt like you didn't exist the next? Remember the boss who has the awful habit of delivering unwarranted sarcasm and underserved negative comments phrased as jokes? Have you ever left a meeting with a boss feeling like you were run over by a train that came out of nowhere? They have an on-purpose agenda that often leaves you feeling stabbed in the back, duped, used, and outwitted.

If you are thinking yes to any of the aforementioned questions, you've experienced a Passive-Aggressive Boss. This boss is a cruel and evil serial killer. Subordinates who work for this boss are left trying to figure out how to best approach him on a regular basis, which essentially lands subordinates in a position where they are forced to manage the manager. Expectations don't exist until they are being yelled and ranted about during one of this boss's episodes because something went wrong. Afterward, he apologizes, which is usually followed by a team compliment.

While all of this is happening, employees are usually not receiving any feedback on their performance and when they do, it's usually based on whatever emotion this boss was experiencing at that time. If passivity is at the core of your boss's management style, don't expect any fair, consistent leadership.

Workers who put forth the bare minimum likely could not care less if the boss has a passive nature. This typically affects high-performing employees who require some nurturing. They deserve a boss who is going to help them be even more efficient and resolve any problems that may arise in a timely manner. Good employees merit a boss who is also in a position to help them get the recognition and rewards they deserve when they go the extra mile.

A manager who vacillates, moves the group in new directions based on new feedback at the drop of a hat, and never seems sure of the appropriate direction will make employees *crazy*! These man-slaughtering bosses push away employees with their insanity of asking them to start, restart, and change direction over and over. Employees do not respect bosses who change direction based on other boss's changing feedback or mood.

You can try to please your boss—and most employees do—but not at the risk of losing your own mind trying to follow or serve someone who has no idea what they are doing. Indecisiveness in leadership translates to incompetence, which doesn't make money, meet business goals, or develop subordinates.

This boss is an expert at figuring out which of your buttons to push to get what he or she wants. They push them over and over, eating away at your confidence, diminishing your sense of identity, and the world somehow becomes centered on their needs and priorities. It isn't a good feeling—ever.

TRUE STORY

Marie was a nice person underneath and in spite of it all. She was also extremely knowledgeable about the ins and outs of the job. Unfortunately, she didn't have the grounding, emotional maturity, or personal discipline to be entrusted to lead other people. This is where so many executives get it wrong: they hire people to be bosses at face value, just because they did the job better than their peers, or because their high energy is something they are hoping will spread. And that simply isn't sound judgment.

She freaked out about everything, and I do mean *everything*—it was like a roller coaster ride with her every day. When I worked for her, I recognized this personality right away, and I dealt with her accordingly. I put my emotions aside; I didn't take her emotional outbursts seriously. Anything important I would e-mail her about, keeping good records. I stayed professional at all times.

Staying professional was a bit challenging, because this boss type is infamous for their attempts to "make friends" with their subordinates, which is a part of their manipulative tactics. When you view them as a friend, you're more likely to excuse bad behaviors or brush them off as them having a bad day.

She would always try to bait me into personal conversations in an effort to connect so she could spew her abuse. Even if a problem arose in my daily duties, I would communicate immediately and let her know my plan of action to resolve, so I could douse her freak-out reaction. She would usually just repeat my plan to resolve and impress upon me the importance of making sure I get it done so I don't create any other issues.

I could sense she hated that I had no emotional reaction to her outbursts. I simply refused to participate in her addiction to freak everyone out and then calm everyone down. It's important to note here that while I was able to deal with this, not everyone will have this ability and they shouldn't be expected to.

Working with her manager to manager was an entirely different experience. It distanced our interaction a ton. We did have to interact in management meetings, which could easily happen a few times a week. Now I witnessed this serial killer boss personality in a different light.

She would kidnap our management meetings with her projection of how one or more of our processes are flawed and could cause something catastrophic unless someone did something about it. Most times the majority vote was less extreme and emotional, and she'd usually transition into Positive Polly who's just happy to be here, have a job, loves her team so much, and would do whatever needs to be done to help any of them out. Not surprisingly, her behaviors were never addressed, or probably even recognized. I can say that with certainty because she never changed.

"I cannot trust a man to control others who
cannot control himself."

—*Robert E. Lee*

INTERVIEW RECAP WITH AVI
BEST/WORSE BOSS INTERVIEW
EMILY VS. JAMES

Best: My best teacher was Ms. Jones. She explained her instructions, and her tone was calm, yet firm. She took the time to listen to students' inquiries and questions. She stayed on topic and didn't ever veer off point. Always willing to help, very approachable, knowledgeable. She admitted when didn't know something, and she promised to research it and get back with you.

Worse: My worst teacher was Mr. Jefferson. He cuts you off when you're speaking. He doesn't explain instructions and doesn't listen to his students. He assumes things; he doesn't seem to care about his students. He is mean, and makes you feel like there is no point in asking a question. He is unfair and throws tantrums in the classroom. Discriminates between students and yells at you when you don't understand or get an answer wrong. He ignores students when he's in a mood; he also acts one way with students (negative) and acts different (more positive) when other teachers/faculty are around.

Notice this thirteen-year-old didn't say her teacher was the best because she gave them candy or let them have recess and an extra ten minutes—nor did she describe her worst teacher as the worst because he didn't do these things. Her observations were based on their ability and follow-through to listen, answer questions, be approachable, be honest, and be their authentic selves.

In other words: to teach her academically and in character.

She values a teacher who embodies integrity and helps their students when they need it. You must see the validity in this student's observation. Your child's academic fate is hugely dependent upon the teacher they are required to submit to, just as an employee's professional success is hugely impacted by whom they are required to submit to. When company owners and schools become aware of this, fully convinced that it is a problem within their leadership, and take action, we can all finally start working together to make the workplace and school better. Employees and students have the right to learn and work in a place that supports their growth as opposed to being thrust into a place where they are abused, knowingly or unknowingly.

THE FIX

For the boss who sees him or herself in this chapter, awareness is half the battle. Do your self-work to improve, like reading blogs and books on how to be a better boss. Propose leadership training for you and your peers. Your boss may appreciate your initiative, and oblige. More than anything, start paying close attention to your day-to-day actions and interactions and check yourself.

As an employee, this is a pickle of a situation to navigate through; I personally would start preparations to leave this manager. In the event that doesn't happen quickly for you or you just can't leave right away for other reasons, here are some helpful tidbits:

- Stay professional.

- Try not to take their behavior personally.

- Get everything you can in writing.

- Stand up for yourself, respectfully—not emotionally.

- Refresh your résumé and start searching.

"Your talent and skills can only take you so far. It is your character and values that will sustain you."

—*Iyanla Vanzant*

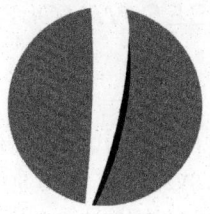

CHAPTER EIGHT

Let's Make It Better—Together

*"In the end, it is important to remember
we cannot become what we need to be by
remaining what we are."*

—Max DePree

Serial killer bosses are everywhere—schools, daycares, restaurants, law enforcement, coffee shops, retail stores, banks, hospitals, warehouses, families, car dealerships, insurance companies, military, entertainment business—you name it. So what does that mean for us? In a nutshell, it means more pain. Pain that will manifest itself in countless ways through countless people over and over until the end of time.

Some people decide to murder their bad leader by giving them poor performance in return, or pay the abuse forward and hurt other innocent people. Some people shut down inwardly and change into a bitter person right before our eyes, while others continue to jump ship in search of the right fit, all the while appearing unstable to onlookers.

I've shined a light on several bad boss behaviors. I've shared real-life experiences, and I've also mentioned several nuggets of wisdom throughout these chapters. But it can't stop here. We have to push this issue, open the conversation worldwide around this epidemic, and then we have to act.

Trust me when I tell you, this subject is personal to me. I have had my share of bad bosses; I didn't understand why it kept happening to *me*, before I learned my purpose. I wouldn't dare end this book without giving you a sneak peek at one of my proprietary training systems. It is so important that today's leaders get the attention and training they need. It's time they see themselves for who they are, and to make a personal commitment to being a better leader than they have been. A great starting point is character development, which I teach through my original 8-Figure Process—a course I strongly suggest be taken by all those who lead people in any form.

It is critical we start being proactive, not reactive in leadership.

To know me is to know that anything I'd ever do or implement has definitive meaning and strategic purpose. What does this 8-Figure Process mean and what's strategic about it? The number *eight* represents going the extra mile, beyond what is natural or comfortable. We all know that seven represents completion, in several different cultures and past studies. If we can be complete in seven steps, why go eight? If you have to ask that, your inquiry alone reveals the need to go eight. Visually speaking, the number *eight* represents a never-ending, through-the-loop, repetitive journey. For instance, we can write the number *eight*, retracing it multiple times if we wanted without our pencil ever leaving the paper. So why would a leader need to go beyond what is natural or comfortable in order for people to do what is asked of them or what they are being paid to do? To that I'll answer you with a question: why wouldn't they? In a millennium world where people are more distracted than ever, why wouldn't a leader go beyond what is comfortable to develop and retain great people, all while protecting the brand of their organization?

As leaders, we have to learn to think, expect, and envision outside of normal if we plan to consistently grow and excel as bosses. Hence the need to innovate and trust a process you may not completely understand or believe in. Is there a limit to what you will do to see your business live, generate lucrative income, provide jobs, attract investors, create a legacy, and leave behind an inheritance for your family?

My 8-Figure Process is an understanding and continuous action of going beyond what is natural or comfortable, for the purpose of achieving desirable results. Let's take a look at the eight key components that make up my 8-Figure Process.

KIMBRETTA'S 8-FIGURE PROCESS

1. Respect
2. Trust
3. Support
4. Knowledge

5. Follow-through
6. Train/mentor
7. Reward
8. (Easy to) Approach

It's important to note that each of these eight components live on a foundation called *communication*. You cannot be successful at doing any of these actions without being an effective communicator both verbally and non-verbally—as an initiator and as a fluid, natural reaction. These elements have to become who you are, and then you have to teach and require these same eight principles to those you lead.

In other words, be what you expect to receive from those around you. When you show up for your people, they will show up for you.

Respect begets respect, trust begets trust, and support begets support. This isn't a magic potion or formula for success—this is doing the right thing over and over and over, in spite of how you feel, who you know, who you like, and no matter the cost.

Be a person of character.

If a person doesn't trust you, they probably don't respect you. If an employee doesn't feel like they have your support, they probably don't trust you. If you have no knowledge of the vision or job you are in charge of, then more times than not, people will not support your ideas or methods. If someone doesn't respect you, chances are they won't be following through on their obligations to you—or doing it poorly at best. If you don't take the time to train the people you have leadership over, you not only risk costly errors, but you also lose any chance of gaining respect or building your subordinates' confidence in you.

The worst part is that you won't have any idea what's going on around you. Can you see how this continuous 8-Figure Process could go in your favor or not?

"The measure of a man's character is what he would do if he knew he never would be found out."

—*Thomas Macaulay*

I once read a quote from Doug Baldwin of the Seattle Seahawks, where he said about his head coach: "We would run through a wall for him." Who on your team, or in your life, would run through a wall for you? Would your employee, your spouse, your friend, or your child run through a wall for you? Even if they would, are they strong enough to run through a wall?

Have you empowered them, encouraged them, and showed up for them enough to build that type of strength and momentum within them? Based on your interactions with them thus far in your relationship, would they even believe they could run through a wall for you if they had to? Have you made enough deposits to their confidence bank to allow such a huge withdrawal of power and assurance? Maybe, maybe not. As an individual, you represent life, and we can't wage financial success, heart, or our life on a *maybe*.

We have to be sure we're repeating actions, habits, and processes that are healthy, boasting positive returns. Developing people takes time and consistency; there will never be a ninety-day or six-month probationary formula, training session, or process to perfect a person's work ethic and character.

Let's destroy these awful leadership practices that have completely defiled our relationships, businesses, finances, and our personal growth. Let's come out! Let's own who we really are as leaders, who we aren't, who we want to be, what we need to learn, and let's work together to make it better.

Everyone wants the world to be a better place, but no one wants to start with self to make that happen. Any change you deem necessary in the world, on your jobs, within your families, will always start with *you*. There is always something you can do within your own self to provoke change. Each one touch one. We are infectious beings—what we do, what we say, and what we believe are extremely contagious.

The power and ability to ignite a better tomorrow has always lived inside of each and every one of us. Dreamers, innovators, and subject matter experts all over the world have started businesses, written books and blogs, and started web series, radio shows, and organizations to help people resolve some sort of problem, to disseminate knowledge, to infect hope, to inspire happiness, and to make our world a better place.

Different people will be attracted to different people, companies, and methodologies, and that's okay. There is plenty of work to go around. I've embarked upon my own very personal dream to transform workplaces into environments where people can wake up and go that will embody a culture of respect, support, growth opportunities, and integrity.

But my dream was suffocated by bad bosses, and at times, it felt like they were out to keep me down. Everything I've been through, every loss, every struggle, and every disappointment has prepared me for this *win*—and I don't take it lightly.

I'm the Bad Boss Destroyer and your next best decision. I'm here to avenge the abused employee, and I won't stop fighting for them.

"The world is a dangerous place to live, not because of the people who are evil, but because of the people who don't do anything about it."

—Albert Einstein

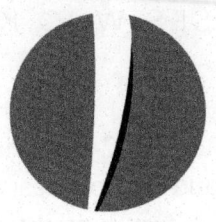

AFTERWORD

"Progress is impossible without change, and those who cannot change their minds cannot change anything."

—George Bernard Shaw

Sent: Thursday, October 10, 2013
From: Kimbretta Clay
Subject: Farewell
Hello, Professional Pals!

It is with bittersweet emotions wherewith I type my last e-mail to most of you. Bitter because I will miss seeing your faces, working with you, our lunch dates, and sharing our humorous reflections on the ups and downs of our profession. Sweet because my future is super bright—I have so many great things to learn and accomplish professionally! It has been my pleasure to not only work with you, but to know you, and I pray that each of you will experience the fullness life has to offer.

I know a lot of you will totally miss my "Quote of the Day" e-mails; so here's one for the road ahead:

"When one door of happiness closes, another one opens: but we often look so long at the closed door that we do not see the one which has been opened for us." —Helen Keller

Thank you,
Kimbretta Clay
Supervisor

We were told on September 24 that our supervisor positions were being eliminated and that our last day would be October 15. As you can see above, my e-mail was sent on October 10. They sent our managers around to each of us that day to "ask" us if we'd like to just go ahead and leave then and that we'll still be paid through the fifteenth.

Just like that.

When I sent this e-mail, I knew I was supposed to write this book. I had been researching to do so for a year. I knew I wanted to start my own business as well. I had just incorporated my company name the previous May, and I had been jotting down ideas and plans for the last two years leading up to that day. Of course, I assumed I had time to pursue my dream in an organized and financially comfortable fashion. I'd take the three-to-five-year-plan route and just keep working and invest time after work for the dream. I would apply a portion of my monthly bonus earnings to funding my dream, which I had been doing. However, this unexpected blow certainly altered that plan.

"To every thing there is a season, a time to
every purpose under the heaven."

—*Ecclesiastes 3:1 (NKJV)*

I was hurt, because I knew it wasn't as simple as them eliminating our positions; they made no effort to move us into another role, nor was there any remorse in the delivery of the news. Once again, in my so-called career, I had been treated as expendable. We were told the organization was going in a new direction. The new direction did not include supervisors. The organization believed the managers could manage the business reports and the subordinates. I sent that e-mail to my colleagues, as that was my character to do so; I even included my bosses and though I left them with that quote, it was really for me. I had to see it, say it, and hear it. I had to be sure I did not miss the door that had been opened for me by being angry, playing the helpless victim, or looking back at the closed door for too long. This was a blessing, an opportunity in work clothes. I had work to do, and now was the time for me to pursue my dreams full force.

So less than one month after my second divorce, I had lost my job. Better stated: my job had lost me. Here I was a single mother, unemployed, and wondering how I would take care of my daughter. These back-to-back circumstances hit hard. For the first time in my life, I was receiving unemployment and I had to apply for food stamps. I felt so low. It was during this period that I began to doubt myself, to be afraid and contemplate taking my own life. This is the part of the rise that is rarely shared: you will experience upset in pursuit of your purpose.

I'm sharing this personal background snippet to really drive home the fact that loyalty no longer exists in the workforce, if it ever did. We are seeing people in authority who are not caring, they do not protect, they do not serve, and they do not develop their subordinates for greater purposes. Business is not people—it's numbers. As a result of that reality, the people who go to work every day and sacrifice their personal dreams to help achieve the dreams of someone else, sacrifice their hobbies, vacations, and relationships in the name of doing a good job and to earn money to pay their bills—these people seemingly always get the short end of the stick.

Seemingly because sometimes what appears to be a setback is just an opportunity to propel you forward. The truth is, I wasn't satisfied at that job and hadn't been for quite some time. I wanted more. I wanted to do work that I believed in, that truly served people and changed lives. I had become fed up with working with bad bosses and seeing them in action day after day. Every day I came to work witnessing people being talked down to, set up for failure, sent into battle with no weapons, and being placed on disciplinary action for nothing short of not being liked. Seeing people brought in and promoted because of who they knew, being forced to deny employees' raises or give them poor raises, being forced to push people out, and witnessing the underhanded tactics of HR—observing these behaviors tore away at my soul. Nonetheless, I was sick of this culture and I wanted it to change.

Hence the idea and vision behind my own business: building a company that would train bosses to be effective, to engage with their employees, and to be leaders of integrity. I had been the employee. I have been the coach, confidant, trainer, interviewer, interviewee, the boss who hired, and the boss who fired. I had seen leadership done all wrong and sometimes done right.

Leadership done right always motivated me, and seeing it done wrong had always angered me. Finally acknowledging those strong, immediate emotions would ultimately provoke me to action. All the time I'd spent working for other companies and other people, unbeknownst to me at the time, had gained me far more than a paycheck. I had found my passion amidst all the hoopla; I'd discovered what I could do to contribute to the resolution. Here I was with nothing but time and opportunity to do just that—establish a company that would contribute to the resolution.

I was scared, yet confident. I knew this wouldn't be easy, but I also knew that no one could give what I had to give the way I would give it to our country's extremely masked, lethal leadership epidemic.

I knew I could make an impact within our society, and I was more than motivated to do so.

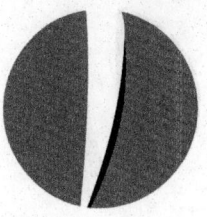

ACKNOWLEDGMENTS

Thank you to my Creator for giving me purpose. Thank you to my only child, my favorite daughter, for inspiring me. Thank you to my editor Shayla for your magic—you gave my voice form and clarity, and I appreciate you. Thank you to my awesome book designer Melinda, for being in the moment. Thank you to my future clients for trusting me to transform your lives. Last but not least, thank you to my readers. A book doesn't breathe until it's read, so thank you for giving my book life.

I would like to acknowledge the people who have prayed for me and believed in me—you know who you are. I hope I inspire the leader in each of you. This is only the beginning, so I hope you all are ready for the journey!

Oh, and, Friend, I still have that journal. Every idea I have gets written on those pages, and I still have empty pages waiting to be filled with more dreams and goals. Thank you.

"You don't need a title to be a leader."

—Anonymous

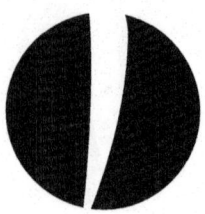

ABOUT THE AUTHOR

Kimbretta Clay is the founding visionary of KayAvi Press Publishing Company. She is also a certified life coach and United States Navy Veteran. Kimbretta's passion for helping others has afforded her the opportunity to manage people at various leadership levels for over twenty years. She has an uncanny ability to bring order to chaos and she can help your company grow via her innovative training methods.

Follow her daily happenings
on Twitter or Instagram
@kimbretta

Visit her website at
kimbretta.com

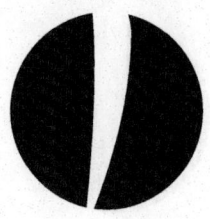

ABOUT THE BOOK

You may think you can keep your work life separate from your personal life, but when serial killer bosses attack you psychologically, it spills over into every area of your life. It's a double whammy—they kill you at work and they torture you at home.

There truly are managers who will push people to make them react negatively. Although we'd like to think that the people we report to at work are well-adjusted, generally happy, and mentally healthy individuals, we sometimes realize that this just isn't so.

There had been moments during Kim Clay's 9-to-5 career when she'd be happy, skipping through the tulips, and then—boom! An awful boss ambushes her, knocking the happy right out of her skip.

We've all been there.

In *Bosses Who Kill*, serial killer bosses are exposed so they can no longer hide behind their job titles as justification for abusing others. This book is for business owners who employee bosses, for those who work for a bad boss, and bad bosses themselves.

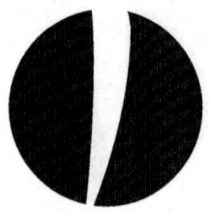

RESOURCES

(Endnotes)

1. Netscape, "No. 1 Reason People Quit Their Jobs." http://webcenters.netscape.compuserve.com/whatsnew/package.jsp?name=fte/quitjobs/quitjobs. Accessed on October 24, 2016.

2. Shirley Lynn Scott, "What Makes Serial Killers Tick?" Accessed on September 13, 2016. http://fc.nghf.dk/~mjo/eng/What+Makes+Serial+Killers+Tick.pdf.

3. F. John Reh, "Top 10 New Manager Mistakes." Accessed September on 28, 2016. https://www.thebalance.com/top-new-manager-mistakes-2275724.

4. WBI 2003 Abusive Workplaces Survey, "Top 25 Workplace Bullying Tactics." Accessed on September 28, 2016. http://www.workplacebullying.org/top-25/.

5. Sherri Gordon, "8 Signs Your Boss Is a Bully." Accessed on September 28, 2016. https://www.verywell.com/signs-your-boss-is-a-bully-460785.

6. Neel Burton, "The Psychology of Laziness." Accessed on September 28, 2016. https://www.psychologytoday.com/blog/hide-and-seek/201410/the-psychology-laziness.